Anonymus

# The bread of forgiveness

A narrative

Anonymus

**The bread of forgiveness**
*A narrative*

ISBN/EAN: 9783742801241

Manufactured in Europe, USA, Canada, Australia, Japa

Cover: Foto ©Andreas Hilbeck / pixelio.de

Manufactured and distributed by brebook publishing software
(www.brebook.com)

Anonymus

**The bread of forgiveness**

# THE

# BREAD OF FORGIVENESS;

## A NARRATIVE.

Blessed are the merciful : for they shall obtain mercy.—
FIFTH BEATITUDE.

———

NEW YORK.
P. O'SHEA, PUBLISHER.
27 BARCLAY STREET.

THE

# BREAD OF FORGIVENESS.

THE city of Pisa was in a state oɪ rejoicing; the bells of the eighty
churches and chapels mingled
their silvery and sonorous voices, and
rang the *Alleluia,* in various joyous
tones, while the two shores of the Arno
which divides the city were crowded with
eager citizens dressed in their holiday
clothes, displaying all the lively spring
colors. The little republic, which was so
often redoubtable to Florence and Genoa,
her haughty rivals, was rejoicing over
the return of one of her dearest sons, who
had spread far and wide the commerce
and increased the wealth of his coun-

try Pietro Gambacorti at last camc
back to Pisa, after a long sojourn in
foreign countries; he had visited France,
then a prey to civil wars; Flanders, so
brilliant, owing to the industry and intel-
ligence of her courageous inhabitants;
England, flourishing within, and victorious without; Spain and that cherished
city of the Moors, beautiful Granada,
the shores of Africa, the Grecian islands,
and Byzantium, which had not as yet
fallen under the yoke of the Ottomans;
but during his long journeys, he had
never forgotten his country, and he had
everywhere sought to extend her commerce, and spread her renown. Thus
although he was absent, his name, long
since popular, had remained familiar
and dear to his fellow citizens; and
when the galley, adorned with his arms,
stopped at the great marble quay which
confined the blue waters of the Arno,
when Pietro Gambacorti descended and

set his foot upon the cherished land of Pisa, prolonged acclamàtions greeted his appearance. The magistrates advanced and complimented him; the numerous clients of his house followed him, uttering loud huzzas; his family and friends surrounded him, congratulating him, and accompanied by this mingled suite, he reëntered his ancestral home, situated near the Church of the Knights. His wife, pale with emotion, came joyfully to meet him; she, too, was followed by a sweet and touching train; seven children surrounded their mother, and cast respectful looks upon the traveler. He embraced and blessed them all, from the oldest, Pietro, whose youthful yet serious face bore traces of his vigils and austerities, down to the little Thora, a pretty child of seven years of age, with sweet, innocent eyes, who said, throwing her arms about her father's neck: "You are my father!

our mother has so often told me about you." Then, followed by his family and friends, he appeared upon the balcony of his house, and thanked the people who thronged the streets, and whose joyous cries told of nothing save blessings and good wishes. " In order to prove to you," he said finally, " that my intention is permanently to reside among you, my friends and brethren, I declare that I betroth my daughter Thora, here present, to Simon de Massa, whose father you all well know, and that the festival with which Pisa has greeted me, shall be henceforward (a sacred family anniversary—to us all."*

So saying he took little Thora's hand, placed it in that of Simon, a fine youth of fourteen years, who looked proudly and lovingly upon his sweet and charm-

* Pietro Gambacorti, surnamed *Peter of Pisa*, is ranked by the Church among the beatified. He was the founder of the Hermitage of St. Jerome.

ing betrothed. The two families applauded, the people redoubled their acclamations; Thora, alone, grew pale, as if the noise and tumult of the multitude, somewhat to be dreaded, even when friendly in its tone, had frightened her; but when Simon, urged on by her father, leaned forward to embrace her, she innocently turned her cheek towards him, saying:

"I will beg God to give me the grace to love you, if I am to be your wife."

"Will that be a hard task for you?" asked Simon.

"I do not know, if God wills it!"

Just then the popular shouts, the noisy blessings of the crowd, which rather resembled threats, the sight of so many heads, like to the waves of a swelling sea, so terrified the young betrothed that she fled for refuge to her mother's arms. The latter saw no better remedy for her fears than to lead her within doors, give her her supper, and put her to bed, whilst the Massa and Gambacorti families drained several flagons in honor of the alliance which was to unite their children.

## II.

YEARS passed on. Pietro Gambacorti raised to the rank of Lord and Captain General of the Pisan republic, was busied in maintaining and extending his power, and in firmly establishing in his house that fleeting authority, which, at the time of which we are treating, in all the Italian cities, passed from hand to hand, from faction to faction. He had numerous friends, still more numerous clients; but amid his most intimate friends and most devoted adherents, he specially distinguished Jacopo Cappiano, who had accompanied him in his distant journeys, who was his partner, his confident, and whom he loved like a brother. Whilst he was wholly occu-

pied with earthly things, a flower for
the heavenly gardens was growing up
within his house. Thora, Simon's betrothed, was one of those favored beings
who keep their baptismal innocence
until death; brought up in the bosom
of a proud family, hearing of naught
save war and ambitious projects, she
had remained humble, simple and gen-
tle; she dearly loved God, and after
Him, she loved only her relatives and
the poor, those privileged friends of
Jesus Christ. While yet very young,
she might be seen daily praying for
whole hours before the tabernacle, and
sighing at the sight of the little golden
door not yet opened for her; her great-
est reward, her most anxiously sought
pleasure, that which she obtained from
her father by means of tender caresses,
was to go to visit the poor and the sick,
to carry them alms, less precious than
the loving smiles which accompanied

them. The festivals of the Gamba-
,corti palace, overwhelmed her with fatigue and sadness; but angelic joy
shone in her face when she approached
the wretched. She did more than assist them, she loved them; and I know
not what science of the heart inspired
her with consoling words, which raised
their souls above earth, and taught them
to bear resignedly the weight of the
cross. All were amazed at such pre-
cocious wisdom, and Thora's companions related with mingled fear and admi-
ration, that, like St. Elizabeth of Hun-
gary, she had a special predilection for
lepers, and that they had seen her kneel
down to wash and kiss their sores.
" *What will become of that child?*" was
the general question; and Simon de
Massa was delighted by these praises,
for he loved Thora, and impatiently
awaited the time fixed upon for their
nuptials.

The days wore on. Thora was almost
fifteen years old, and her next birthday
was to be that of her marriage. She
was making due preparation for it by
imploring of God the graces which make
chaste wives and blessed mothers, when
her young betrothed died suddenly.
His death overwhelmed both families
with grief. Thora also wept for him,
for she loved him like a brother, and in
her quiet yet deep sorrow, she realized
that her earthly ties were broken. The
Lord called her to himself, and, conse-
crated to him alone, she was no more
to serve the ambitious views of her family. Widow and virgin at the same
time, she willingly renounced the world,
and sought by some external mark to
make her secret wishes and intentions
known to her parents. She cut off her
long hair, laid by her silken and fine
woolen garments, which had long con-
cealed a hair cloth, and appeared thus

clad, in the midst of her family, who were already arranging a new alliance for her.

"You weep for your husband, my daughter," said Pietro Gambacorti. "I also have wept with you; but another quite as rich and loving seeks you in marriage, and ere many months, will lead you to the altar."

She shook her head and answered: "Another, in fact, calls me to himself, but it is no mortal spouse; another seeks your alliance: do not reject him, dear father, for that spouse is Jesus Christ himself."

"You wish to become a nun?"

"Yes, my lord and father. And I come to solicit your blessing. You are the one I love best in the world, since my mother is no more; and yet I must leave you, for I have heard the voice which says to those who mourn, *The master is here, and calleth for thee!*"

At these words, uttered with calm resolution, Pietro Gambacorti wept, and his sons exclaimed against them, for their sister's hand was destined to procure them new friends and stronger alliances; but she remained firm against tears, prayers, and even threats, although her tenderness for her relatives caused her to weep bitterly in her turn. She longed, prayed, and struggled, pleading a divine cause against earthly reasons, overcoming her own heart, which also spoke in favor of her relatives, and repeated to her how sweet and powerful were the words of pure love. Days, weeks, and months passed by, before she could obtain her father's consent: but God at last softened his heart, and she was permitted to consecrate herself to God, in a monastery, of the order of St. Dominic, within the very walls of Pisa.

## III.

IT was there that God willed her to
dwell; there it was that she first en-
joyed that inexpressible rest, that
delicious serenity of those souls who feel
themselves in their true vocation, and,
who understand that they obey fully and
unreservedly the designs which Provi-
dence has had over them. That certain-
ty is the first basis of earthly happiness,
or perhaps, even, there is no other felici-
ty to be met with here below. Thora,
or rather Clara, for the daughter of the
Gambacorti family took, in religion, the
name of the humble virgin of Assis-
sium. Clara, in embracing the monastic
life, resembled those exiles, who, after a

long absence, return to their own country; the landscape, the views, the customs are familiar to them; their lips, which stammered foreign tongues, gladly resume their national language; their steps recognize the city paths, they seat themselves by friendly hearths, they salute well-known faces, and their souls, so long closed, are reopened and warmed among their childhood's friends. So it was with Clara. Exiled in the world, a stranger to its ideas, and to its language, she found herself in her true country within those blessed walls, wherein Jesus Christ reigned. All that she saw, all that she heard, was the echo of her own feelings, of her own thoughts; there they loved God, as she wished to see him loved. There they despised the delights of the world which she had known and despised; there they aspired towards heaven, the sole object of her desires and prayers. Good works and

the austerities of penance; those mysterious steps which lead to the celestial
Zion, had nothing to alarm her ever in
creasing fervor. She said with the
Prophet King: "*How lovely are thy
tabernacles, O Lord of hosts!. My soul
longeth and fainteth for the courts of the
Lord. My heart and my flesh have re-
joiced in the living God. For the sparrow
hath found herself a house, and the turtle
a nest for herself where she may lay her
young ones. Thy altars, O Lord of hosts,
my king, and my God!*" And she never grew weary of that abode which she
had chosen as a shelter against the
storms of the world. Her soul, inunda-
ted with the balm of charity, overflowed
like a well filled deep, and shed round
her treasures of compassionate tenderness. Although she was at peace, she
did not forget those who suffered, and
who had always had so large a share in
her affections; she still assisted the

poor by means of the alms which she begged for them; the afflicted sought consolation from her who had received from heaven the gift of happy and consoling words, and her watchful compassion, which forgot none of the human ills, extended itself even over foundlings, then so neglected. She busied herself actively about them, raising up benefactors for them, and succeeded in opening an asylum, for those poor despised and abandoned little beings, which is still in active operation. Like the good angels, Clara never lost sight of God's face, even while exercising works of mercy towards her brethren. Prayer was her strength and her inspiration, and she prepared herself at the foot of the tabernacle, to answer to God, who questions souls by trials and by crosses.

Whilst she lived peaceful and hidden, her country was a prey to bitter dissen-

sions; if, as we have said above, power
passed from hand to hand, in all the
Italian republics, with it also spread the
torch of civil discords. War and enmi-
ty abounded; Pisa and Genoa had
long disputed the empire of the seas;
after the deadly battle of the Meloria,
the vanquished Pisans had been forced
to confine their ambition within their
city walls; but there, the rival factions
contended for supremacy. Foreign ene
mies fixed their eyes upon the fertile
territory of that little republic, upon
that city so rich in sumptuous monu-
ments. Galeazzo Visconti, Duke of
Milan, sought to include it within the
meshes of his conquests, and, if his
soldiers had not yet penetrated into the
inclosure of Pisa, his gold had found
many hands open to receive it. Pietro
Gambacorti thought himself sure of the
power which he had possessed for twen-
ty-four years, and, in his blind confi-

dence, he did not see the enemy of his own race and nation rising up beside him. Appiano, his friend, his adopted son, the sharer of his most secret thoughts, had, for several years, entertained relations with Galeazzo Visconti. Invested with the chief functions of the Pisan republic, full of talent, skill and insinuation, he had succeeded in attaching to himself numbers of followers, and in secretly undermining the power and credit of Gambacorti. Vainly had a devoted friend sought to warn the latter; he only answered shaking his head:

"Appiano will not betray his old friend! I have lived seventy years without mistrust; do not try to shake my faith in friendship."

This noble and generous confidence was betrayed. Secret rumors were spread throughout the city, and had reached the monastery of the "Daugh-

ters of St. Dominic ; " they learned that
the power and perhaps the life of Gambacorti were threatened. Clara, carried
her sorrows and fears to the foot of the
altar. There she tremblingly prostrated herself, her face bathed in tears, and
with the simplicity of a child, confided
her grief to her God. Her father was
the dearest earthly love of her heart,
and she anxiously besought his salvation, and his life.

" O, my God !" said she, " break up
the plots of wicked men ; send your angel
to defend my father. You are all-pow-
erful, dear Lord, you can save him.
Oh ! spare his enemies so great a crime.
My spouse, and my Lord, I know not
how to pray, I am speechless before you,
but you read the depths of my soul ;
you see my anguish. Oh ! take pity on
your poor servant."

Tumultuous cries, which rose from the
street, and penetrated even into the

sanctuary, suddenly interrupted her. She listened, filled with terror. The angry voice of the ocean, the harsh thunders of the stormy clouds, are less terrible than the accent of the angry populace. Clara trembled; she could no longer pray with her lips, but her tears, a more eloquent prayer, told the deep suffering of her soul. She mechanically opened the book lying before her, cast her eyes thereon and read these words: *My enemy hath persecuted my soul; he hath brought down my life to the earth; he hath trodden on me all the day long.* "Alas!" said she, finishing the verse of the psalm; "*Rise up, O Lord, in thine anger, show thy power against mine enemies.*"

A burst of furious cries interrupted her; she looked imploringly at the Tabernacle, and then a second time took up the book. It opened at these words, wherein David complains to the Almighty; "*My enemies are like lions waiting to devour their prey; they are like lions' whelps, hidden in secret places.*"

Though her well balanced mind did not believe in superstitious warnings, however, while reading those words of the Prophet, which applied so well to her father surrounded by enemies, she could not fail to shudder. The cries rose more threatening and implacable; she distinguished these sinister threats. "Death to Gambacorti." "Viva, viva, Appiano!" "Traitor," cried she involuntarily.

But at that very moment she repented these angry exclamations, and prostrating herself upon the sanctuary floor, she sobbed bitterly, washing the marble tiles with her tears. She tried not to hear; but the cries and the sound of the bells which called to arms, unceasingly resounded in her ears, and disturbed the mystic silence of God's house.

"Father, where are you?" she said at last. "What terrible fate awaits your grey hairs! My God! my God, save him, or, if he must fall under the sword of your merciful justice, receive the victim into heaven, and pardon his murderers."

She rose and resolved to go and rejoin her sisters, whom she knew to be greatly alarmed for her, for she was greatly beloved by them. The community were all assembled in a hall just in front of the entrance gate, and all the nuns were praying, some prostrated, some with their arms stretched out in form of a cross, like Moses upon the mountain, and redoubling the fervor of their supplications, according as the tumult without affrighted them. When Clara appeared in their midst, the uproar increased, and cries of, Death! death! kill him, strike! no pardon! terrified those timid virgins. Just then, repeated blows shook the gate. Clara ran thither, and looking through the grating which opened upon the street, saw crowds of people drunk with wine, blood, and fury, pursuing, like a pack of hounds, a man already wounded, who had succeeded in clinging to the bars of the monastery gate. She recognized the man; he was her brother, Lorenzo.

"Asylum!" cried he in a faltering voice, and recognizing Clara, said to her: "Sister, our father has been assassinated by Appiano's emissaries; one of our brothers has perished with him; this ungrateful populace pursues me, and seeks my life; an asylum! sister, an asylum!"

That monastery had not the right of asylum, and the entrance was strictly interdicted to men. The sister portress, however, shook her keys, and said:

"Shall I open it, mother?"

"No," answered Clara; "the door

must remain closed! Lorenzo, I cannot open to you an asylum." *

Lorenzo only answered by a look of resignation, and dropped the door-knocker which he had seized. He withdrew, but the furious horde soon overtook him, and struck him ten mortal blows. Just as he expired, Clara fell like dead into the arms of her distressed sisters.

* Historical. The "Bollandists" remark that Clara could not save her brother's life ; that by opening the doors of her monastery, she would have gravely infringed the rules of her order, and perhaps have exposed the safety of her sisters.

## IV.

**P**IETRO GAMBACORTI and two
of his sons had fallen under the
blows of the perfidious Appiano ; and Clara, pierced to the very
heart, walked rapidly towards the
tomb. The tyrant's hand had struck
her in striking her family. Her body
was weakened under the suffering, but
her mind and memory remained un
shaken, and her sisters perceived that
she had not forgotten the sorrows of
her ancestral home. Whenever they
entered her cell, they always found
her weeping, and casting resigned and
sorrowful looks upon her crucifix.
Death had already spread a livid pale-

ness over her cheeks; but the name of
Appiano, if pronounced before her,
flushed her forehead, and silent indig-
nation shone in her eyes. However,
she never spoke of him herself.
They mourned her approaching death,
for she took no nourishment, and life
seemed ready to take leave of her ex-
hausted body; she thought herself about
to appear in the presence of her sover-
eign Judge, and she asked for the con-
fessor of the monastery. He came; she
confessed long and tearfully, and the
sisters who served her, upon returning
to her cell, wondered that the last con-
fession of so pure and penitential a life,
should be accompanied by such bitter
sorrow. They spoke of it to her.
Clara smiled feebly and begged them to
prepare an altar in her room, wherein
the sacred host, which the priest had
gone to fetch, might repose. Then,
joining her hands, she waited quietly.

The sound of a bell announced the approach of the viaticum for the dying. All the sisters, candle in hand, preceded and followed the divine spouse of their souls; when Clara perceived it, her dying eyes reopened; she raised herself into a sitting posture, and after a momentary silence, she said in a loud and distinct voice:

"Sisters, in presence of my God, whom I am about to receive for the last time in all probability, I declare that I fully and freely forgive Jacopo Appiano, and his followers, the evil which they have done to my family. I forgive him heartily; I renounce all feelings of resentment, and, I pray God to show him mercy, and to assist him. Remember my last words; I have no more enemies on earth."

Upon finishing these words, she cast a calm and loving glance towards the ciborium, and when she had received the bread of life, all noticed that her forehead seemed less pale, and that the signs of approaching death seemed gone from her features. She remained some time plunged in profound recollection ; a peaceful smile enlightened her face ; she rested after her victory, and her soul, calmed by the forgetfulness of injuries, and the sweet influence of mercy, reveled uninterruptedly in the presence of the God of all consolation.

Leaving her somewhat refreshed, the sub-prioress of the monastery came to her and said affectionately :

"You seem better, dear sister, God be praised ! *You will not die, but will live, and will relate the works of the Lord.* We must seek to second God's designs ; will you not try to take a little nourishment ?"

Clara smiled gently, and replied : "I would willingly take some refreshment to strengthen me, but I have a request to make you, regarding it."

"Speak, dear daughter; your wish shall be granted."

"Well, then, I should like you to send in my name to Jacopo Appiano's house, and beg him to send me a dish from his table, as my father did to him. I think that food would cure me."

The sub-prioress's face expressed profound astonishment: "My dear daughter," cried she, "what are you thinking of? Appiano, the murderer! Do not recall those remembrances, sister, they are but too vividly before me. I love those who are dead, better than ever daughter or sister loved; judge, then, what I have felt towards their assassin! but the victorious grace of Jesus Christ has subdued my heart. I wish, like my divine master, to love and to pardon! Alas! why should we hate? we are so short a time on earth. Yes, my daugh-

ter, God reserves vengeance to himself.
Appiano will not escape it. Oh! let
us rather pray that he may repent and
that we may be all reunited in heaven."

At this cry, forced from the saint's
heart, the prioress no longer hesitated;
she saw the divine inspiration in her
request. A messenger was immediately dispatched, who reached Appiano's
house just at dinner-time. He made
known his errand. The new lord of
Pisa was confounded by such unex-
pected words; he turned pale, and remained speechless. His wife burst into
tears and exclaimed:

"Oh, holy and unhappy lady, you
shall be obeyed!"

She immediately filled a basket with
fish, fruit, and bread, and giving it to
the messenger, said to him in an hum-
bled and trembling voice:

"Carry this to the holy lady who
sends you, and say to her that we poor

sinners, most earnestly recommend ourselves to her prayers."

And when he had departed, she said boldly to her silent and terrified husband:

"Oh! Jacopo! what have you done! The daughter of your benefactor!"

"Be quiet," he answered her. "Heaven already avenges them."

They brought Clara what she had requested; she took a piece of bread, and ate it, after making over it the sign of the cross; and that bread which her companions called "*the bread of forgiveness*," seemed to exercise a mysterious virtue over her feeble body. She recovered, she rose from that bed wherein she had languished since the death of her father, and resumed, with increasing fervor, her life of prayer and good deeds. She prayed especially for her dead, and for Appiano, and when they wondered at her constant meditations, her prolonged vigils, and the fatigue, and penances which she imposed upon herself, she merely said to her sisters :

"Oh! watch and pray with me. There are those now upon earth, who will, very shortly, be surprised by the coming of the Son of man. It is a fearful thing to fall into the hands of the living God. Oh! let us pray."

# V

VENGEANCE, even upon earth, is seldom tardy, and frequently the arrow turns back to pierce him who aimed it. The popular favor, as inconstant as thoughtless, turned against Appiano, and he, in his turn, was forced to drink of the chalice which he had prepared for his friend and benefactor. The sedition which he had raised against Gambacorti, came resounding around his palace gates: the cries of death, which he had formerly dictated, now reached his ears, mingled with his own name. The power which he had shaken under another's steps, now crumbled before his feet, and the daggers which he had taught to murder, now threatened his own breast. Treated in his turn as a seditionary and a public enemy; he lost first his power, and then his life.

The servants of the monastery brought this news to Clara; she raised her eyes towards heaven, and said sorrowfully:

"Oh! God! how terrible are thy judgments. I had not asked for his death, but for his conversion; and now, Lord, I implore thee, in thy great mercy, to grant him salvation."

She prayed some moments in silence, during which time a religious inquired the fate of the wife and daughters of Appiano.

"They are wandering about Pisa, threatened by an angry crowd, and find no one, even among the warmest partisans of Appiano, who is willing to give them shelter. They all dread the fury of the exasperated people, who have

just learned that he intended to sell
Pisa to the Duke of Milan. They are
penniless; their palace has been pil-
laged, their wealth seized, and their
friends murdered, or put to flight. Let
them come here," cried Clara. "The
monastery doors shall be opened for
them; go and seek them; the daughter
of Gambacorti has a right to save the
widow and children of Appiano. Go,
in heaven's name!"

They obeyed that voice which com-
manded with the authority of clemency.
Two devoted servants ran in search of
the fugitives, and in about an hour,
brought the widow and her weeping
daughters to the monastery. Clara
awaited them. Clara took them in her
arms and said to them, with the utmost
sweetness:

. "Here you have nothing to fear."
The house which she had been unable
to open to her own brother, became a

sacred asylum, wherein no one dare pursue the wife and children of the murderer; the anger of the populace subsided before the virtue of Clara, as before an impassable barrier; they no longer dared hate those whom she pardoned.

The faithful servant of God, who had learned to immolate at the foot of the cross, her hatred and desire for vengeance, received, even in this life, the recompense of her virtues, for her love of God daily increased, and she finished her long and saintly life, in the continual exercise of good works. Her soul was in peace with all creatures; her life was calm, her death happy. She expired at a good old age, surrounded by her sisters, watching joyfully for the approach of the spouse who came to seek her, and saying:

"Come, Lord Jesus, I wait for thee, behold me on the cross."

It was the 17th of April, 1419.

Her life and death verified the holy words of the Beatitudes pronounced upon the mountain; "Blessed are the merciful, for they shall obtain mercy."

www.ingramcontent.com/pod-product-compliance
Lightning Source LLC
Chambersburg PA
CBHW032142080426
42733CB00008B/1176